Contents

Acknowledgments

The Central Office of Information would like to thank NCVO (National Council for Voluntary Organisations), the TUC and the Department of the Environment for their co-operation in compiling this book.

Cover Photograph Credit
Greenpeace/Morris.

Introduction

This book describes the full range of pressure groups in Britain,[1] including promotional pressure groups and sectional pressure groups or interest groups. It outlines their historical development and gives a detailed account of the important part they play in Britain's system of government at both local and national levels. It describes their methods of campaigning, including lobbying and the use of publicity—a detailed case study of the campaign against lead in petrol illustrates this, while a wide range of examples of other pressure groups is also provided. The book also describes the international role of some pressure groups and their activities within the European Union.

Information on closely related themes is available in some of the other titles in the Aspects of Britain series, including *Organisation of Political Parties, Parliament* and *The British System of Government*.

---

[1] The term 'Britain' is used informally in this book to mean the United Kingdom of Great Britain and Northern Ireland; 'Great Britain' comprises England, Wales and Scotland.

What are Pressure Groups?

Accounts of how Britain is governed often centre on the election of Members of Parliament (MPs) and the policies of the parties to which they belong—on the creation of laws, and their implementation by Government. However, British citizens have other ways—apart from elections to Parliament or local councils—of expressing their views and trying to influence the way their lives are governed.

Many people belong to political parties but millions of people also belong to other organisations which reflect their interests and concerns. In the voluntary sector alone, it is estimated that one-third of the population is involved in regular work for voluntary organisations, many of which are pressure groups. These are organisations which aim to influence Parliament and Government in the way decisions are made and carried out, to the benefit of their members and the cause they support.

Range of Groups

There is a huge range of pressure groups, covering areas such as politics, business, employment, consumer affairs, ethnic minorities, aid to developing countries, foreign relations, education, culture, defence, religion, sport, transport, health, social welfare, animal welfare and the environment. Some have over a million members; others only a few dozen. Some exert pressure on a number of different issues; others are concerned only with a single issue. Some groups have come to play a recognised role in the way Britain is governed; others seek influence through radical protest.

Types of Group

There are various ways of classifying pressure groups, based, for example, on their membership, aims, ways of operating and relationship with the Government. One fairly common way is to distinguish between groups which represent, or act on behalf of, the interests of people in particular sections of society, such as coal miners or doctors; and groups which campaign for a particular issue or cause, such as prison reform or the protection of animals.

Groups in the first category are known as sectional or *interest groups*, and those in the latter as *promotional* or just *pressure groups*. This division is not a rigid one. Some pressure groups start by campaigning about a single issue, and then develop such a large membership and range of concerns that they take on many of the features of interest groups. For example, the Automobile Association (AA) began in 1905 with the single aim of warning motorists about police speed-traps. Today the size of its membership—more than 6 million—is such that it could be seen as an interest group representing British motorists. The Child Poverty Action Group campaigns to relieve poverty among children and families with children. It is usually seen as a promotional group because it campaigns for a particular cause. However, some would argue that it is an interest group, because it acts on behalf of a particular group of people in society. While some pressure groups have a single aim of influencing the Government and public to achieve the changes they want, for others influencing policy is a secondary objective. Their main aim is to provide a social service or help their members to enjoy a pastime.

An interest group, such as a trade union, might act as a single-issue group when it campaigns on an individual cause, such as legislation on safety or Sunday trading. There is, therefore, some justification for a 'hybrid' category for pressure groups which have interest and promotional characteristics. However, for the sake of simplicity, this book will use the promotional/interest distinction.

Charities

There are between 400,000 and 500,000 voluntary organisations in Britain, of which some 170,000 are registered as charities with the Charity Commission for England and Wales, a statutory body which regulates and advises charities. (Scotland and Northern Ireland have different regulatory systems.) To qualify for charitable status, a voluntary organisation's aims must include one of the following:

—the relief of poverty (including sickness and distress);

—the advancement of education;

—the advancement of religion (of whatever faith); or

—the promotion of other certain purposes beneficial to the community (such as good community relations, the prevention of racial discrimination, the protection of health and the promotion of equal opportunities).

Charitable status brings with it considerable advantages: it offers legal protection against abuse, failure and interference. It can inspire public confidence and stimulate donations, and it offers exemption from some forms of direct taxation.

There is a crucial difference between charitable and non-charitable organisations. Non-charitable organisations can support any cause they wish provided they keep within the law. Charities, however, are not allowed to take part in any party political activity. They cannot have political objectives but are constrained by law to the reasoned advocacy of causes which directly further their non-political charitable purposes. They can, however, draw attention to problems which affect their work and can provide information and advice for the Government when requested; they can comment on government proposals for legislation as set out in Green and White Papers and other consultation documents. They can also provide MPs and members of the House of Lords with arguments for or against a Bill; and can seek to persuade MPs to support their charitable purposes.

A charity may not, however, go on improperly to influence the British Government or the government of any other country. Because of these constraints, many self-help groups and campaigning pressure groups do not have charitable status.

Some voluntary organisations set up two separate bodies: one non-charity to act as a pressure group; the other a charity for those activities which fit within the definition of charitable activity.

Other Groups

There is a small but growing category of organisations, often known as 'watchdogs', which have been established in an official or semi-official capacity to monitor a particular area of public life. Some have been established by Act of Parliament, such as the regulatory bodies for the privatised former nationalised industries, which have statutory duties and statutory powers. Although they are not pressure groups, they exert influence on the Government and industries on behalf of the consumer. The Office of Telecommunications (OFTEL) was set up to supervise the industry, maintain competition and promote the interests of consumers. The Office of Gas Supply (OFGAS) was set up to monitor and oversee the gas industry, to investigate complaints and regulate gas charges. In its annual report in 1993, OFGAS criticised British Gas for its policies on price control and small contracts. The statutory Post Office Users' National Council sent two reports to the President of the Board of Trade (the Secretary of State for Trade and Industry), Michael Heseltine, in 1992, expressing reservations over the possible privatisation of the Post Office.

In addition, there is a wide range of non-political and non-economic organisations in Britain, such as clubs, religious denominations, and voluntary groups whose members share the same pastime, have the same religious belief, or seek to help other people. These organisations do not exist primarily to campaign for or against a particular issue, or to represent their members in negotiations with the Government or other sectors of society. However, they may act as pressure groups when an issue which concerns their members is on the public agenda, or when they want to draw attention to something.

For example, the main purpose of an angling club may be to regulate fishing on a particular river, and to organise competitions for its members. But if the pumping of water by the local water company means that the water level is reduced and the stocks of fish are harmed, then the angling club may decide to protest to the water company. Thus it acts as a pressure group. Similarly, while the Church of England is not primarily a pressure group, it may become involved indirectly, or even directly, in seeking to influence public policy. For example, the Church sometimes produces reports on current issues to which it feels it has a contribution to make, such as the problems of inner cities, or nuclear weapons. The conclusions reached by these reports may call for a change in public policy, and so the Church behaves in a similar manner to a pressure group.

Pressure Groups and Policy

Pressure groups operating at a national level have a number of ways of influencing how Britain is governed. Action by them may highlight a particular problem, which is then acknowledged by the Government. Groups whose scale of membership indicates that they are broadly representative in their field may then be consulted by a government department, or take part in Whitehall working groups or advisory councils. If the Government considers that legislation is necessary, then proposals are drafted, which are circulated to interested groups for their comments. Legislation is then put before Parliament, and at various times during the passage of a Bill—especially at the committee stage—pressure groups have opportunities to influence the content of the Bill. Once a Bill becomes an Act of Parliament, it is implemented by the relevant government department. At this stage, too—particularly if the Act includes delegated legislation—pressure groups may be consulted and have the opportunity to provide information and express their views.

Origins of Pressure Groups

The Medieval Guilds

For many centuries people in Britain, particularly those engaged in economic activity, have banded together to represent their interests. During the medieval period there were various kinds of guilds, the earliest of which were the religious guilds, or brotherhoods, which developed under the authority of the Christian church. By the fourteenth century, these religious guilds, whose main concern was the well-being of their members, were well-established.

Merchant and Craft Guilds

Merchant and craft guilds also developed in medieval England from the eleventh century. Merchant guilds were organisations of traders in towns and cities whose main task was to regulate a local trade monopoly. Craft guilds were bodies of master craftsmen, and journeymen—skilled workers who had served an apprenticeship—rather than unskilled labourers. These guilds had their own regulations on wages, training and maintaining the quality of their manufactured products. They usually comprised all the craftsmen in a particular type of industry, such as carpentry or printing, in a town. Their aim was to establish a monopoly of all those involved in a particular craft.

Companies of guilds in the City of London, such as fishmongers and clothworkers, still exist today, although their role is mainly ceremonial. Historians in the nineteenth century believed that trade unions were descended from the craft guilds, but it is more likely that following the Industrial Revolution in Britain, which began in the eighteenth century, and brought about the decline of the traditional crafts, journeymen started to form organisations to protect their interests as employees.

The Interests

The growth of Britain's overseas trade in the seventeenth and eighteenth centuries led to the development of the 'moneyed interest'. This consisted chiefly of the Bank of England, and the East India Company, which traded in India and the Far East, and the South Sea Company, which originally traded in Spanish America. There were also other mercantile groups, such as the Royal African Companies and the West India Interest. They enlisted the support of sympathetic MPs, and held discussions with government departments, in order to defend their interests in foreign trade, particularly over laws and taxes. This period also saw the growth of religious groups which represented the interests of Christians, such as Roman Catholics and Quakers, who did not belong to the established Church of England.

Britain's Industrial Revolution in the eighteenth and nineteenth centuries gave rise to new groups which are closely linked to today's pressure groups. The expansion of transport and communications in the 1830s and 1840s established powerful and wealthy 'interests' based on the industrialists who built Britain's canals and railways. These interests had strong connections with many MPs, and were supported by thousands of shareholders.

Nineteenth-century Sectional Groups

The spread of education, developments in health care, and the expansion of manufacturing industry led to the formation of bodies to represent non-manual and industrial workers. Doctors and teachers were just some of Britain's professional workers who formed early pressure groups. The British Medical Association (BMA) was formed in 1832 to represent doctors. It campaigned for medical reform, and sought to make its views known when Parliament discussed medical issues. The National Union of Teachers (NUT—formed 1870) worked to obtain better conditions for teachers, and to influence the making of laws about education.

In the late eighteenth and early nineteenth centuries, groups of craftsmen formed unions to deal with wages and working conditions, entry to their trades, and provision of benefits for sickness, accidents and burial. The unskilled or semi-skilled workers of the new industrial age, for example those in transport or the factories, began to form unions from the mid-nineteenth century.

Development of Peak Groups

The first Trade Union Directory, published in 1861, listed organisations including, for example, the Amalgamated Society of Engineers (founded 1851), and United Operative Stone Masons of Scotland. The chief concerns of trade unions in the nineteenth century were socio-economic—such as the pay, conditions, hours of work and accommodation of the workers they represented—rather than political. The Trades Union Congress (TUC), the 'peak', or representative, organisation for British unions, met annually from 1868. Unions catering for white-collar workers (or office staff) in government, banking and other services became well established from the 1890s onwards.

Employers also banded together in single-industry organisations such as the Shipbuilding Employers' Federation, which was set up in 1889. A national organisation of employers started in 1898. In 1915, the National Association of British Manufacturers was established, followed by the Federation of British Industries (1916), and the British Employers' Confederation (1919). These three bodies merged in 1965 to form the Confederation of British Industry (CBI)—the main peak organisation representing the British business community.

Nineteenth-century Single-issue Groups

The nineteenth century also saw the development of groups which campaigned about specific issues, for example, against slavery or cruelty to animals. These groups made their views known in a number of ways, such as publishing pamphlets, holding public meetings and organising petitions. The most famous single-issue group was the Anti-Corn Law League, set up in 1838 to overturn legislation that protected the price British farmers received for their wheat. The League succeeded in its aims when the Corn Laws were repealed in 1846, despite strong pressure from the influential farming lobby.

Politics and the Unions

Around the end of the nineteenth century, the trade unions began to seek to represent their interests at a political level, an activity which other interest groups, representing trade, industry and the professions, had been involved in for some time. The Labour Party was formed in 1906 as the political wing of the Labour movement, to give the trade unions in particular a voice in politics. Some unions started sponsoring Labour MPs by providing them with financial support, a practice which continues today with many MPs receiving trade union contributions towards their election expenses and the running of their constituency parties. Between 1900 and 1925, trade union membership grew from 12 per cent to 45 per cent of the British workforce, although by 1933 it had fallen back to 22 per cent.

Government and Sectional Groups

The crises of the first half of the twentieth century—the two world wars and the economic depression of the 1930s—led to the Government actively seeking the co-operation of sectional pressure groups. Trade unions were given increased rights in negotiations and brought into the decision-making work of government departments. In Britain's coalition government during the second world war, the trade union leader Ernest Bevin was appointed Minister of Labour. This allowed greater contact between the Government and the unions, as well as a greater role for union representatives on Whitehall committees, which continued after the war. British industrialists were given an advisory role in certain areas of trade policy. For example, the Federation of British Industries was represented on the Import Duties Advisory Committee.

The Rise of Sectional Groups

The period after 1945 saw a continued growth in the role and power of sectional pressure groups. Trade union membership (TUC-affiliated and unaffiliated) grew steadily from 7.9 million in 1945 to 13.3 million in 1979, when the union members affiliated to the TUC formed 52 per cent of the workforce. In 1969, the unions were instrumental in securing the Labour administration's abandonment of legisative reform of industrial relations. The CBI's campaign is often credited with preventing legislation based on the 1977 Bullock inquiry on industrial democracy, particularly trade union representation on company boards in the private sector.

Tripartism

In 1962 the Macmillan administration established the National Economic Development Council (NEDC) to stimulate growth in the economy. The NEDC was a 'tripartite' body; that is, its membership comprised representatives from the trade unions and the employers, and the government; it also included some independent members. It was abolished in 1992.

Other major national public bodies were created by the Government in the 1970s with a 'tripartite' membership that included trade union and employer representatives. The Manpower Services Commission (since abolished) was given responsibility for employment training and placement. The Health and Safety Commission was set up with responsibility for regulating health and safety in places of work. The Advisory, Conciliation and Arbitration Service (ACAS) was established to help settle industrial relations disputes.

The Agriculture Act 1947 is a well-known example of how this changed relationship was given a statutory basis in the post-war period. The Act stated that the minister 'shall consult' with the representative bodies of agricultural producers. In particular, the National Farmers' Union—which represents farmers rather than farm employees—has had a close working partnership with the Ministry of Agriculture, Fisheries and Food.

Today the relations of sectional groups with the Government of the day are less prominent or formalised. At the same time trade union membership fell steadily to 9.5 million by the end of 1991.

Growth of Promotional Groups

There has been a rapid growth in the number of promotional pressure groups since the end of the second world war, especially those campaigning on issues relating to consumer affairs, the environment and social conditions. A random survey of 10 per cent of the approximately 2,000 groups listed in *The Voluntary Agencies Directory* showed that 75 per cent had been formed since 1950, and over 50 per cent since 1970.

Developments since the 1950s

In the late 1950s the Consumers' Association was formed to uphold the rights of consumers, and the Campaign for Nuclear Disarmament (CND) started as a protest movement against nuclear weapons. In the 1960s the formation of groups such as the Child Poverty Action Group, and the housing organisation, Shelter, highlighted growing concern over social issues. By the 1960s ownership of television in Britain was widespread, and pressure groups were able to make effective use of this and the other media in communicating their message. The 1970s and 1980s saw growing support for groups concerned with environmental issues, such as Greenpeace and Friends of the Earth, and human rights—for example, Amnesty International. The growing numbers of nuclear weapons on both sides of the Iron Curtain in the late 1970s and early 1980s led to the formation of new pacifist groups, and there was a revival in the fortunes of CND, with its number of recorded supporters rising to more than 100,000 by the early 1980s.

The major charity fund-raising events of the 1980s, such as Band Aid, Sport Aid, and other appeals for aid to parts of the world affected by famine and disasters, made innovative use of the international mass media. The prime objective was to mobilise support and raise funds on a massive scale, and the sheer size of the events, involving millions of people worldwide, brought the issues of famine and development to the attention of politicians and the public. The increasing prominence of minorities in British society was also reflected in the formation and growth of pressure groups representing ethnic and sexual minorities, as well as support groups for people with particular illnesses or other problems, and their dependants.

Pressure Groups Today

Sectional or Interest Groups

Interest groups, which represent the interests of a particular sector of society, operate mainly in industry, commerce, finance and the professions. Their role is to campaign on behalf of their members, either in relation to employers or other sectional groups, or in relation to the Government or the European Union (EU). Membership is normally restricted to people who work in the relevant section.

Confederation of British Industry

A large number of sectional groups belong to what are sometimes called 'peak' groups, which represent their section as a whole. More than 250,000 public and private companies are members of the CBI, as are more than 150 trade associations, employers' organisations and their member companies. Members of the CBI employ about half Britain's workforce. The CBI, which describes itself as an independent, non-party political organisation, states that 'it exists primarily to voice the views of its members to ensure that governments of whatever political complexion—and society as a whole—understand both the needs of British business and the contribution it makes to the well-being of the nation'.

The CBI is represented on the British Overseas Trade Board. It nominates members to ACAS and the Health and Safety Commission (HSC), and members of the Commission for Racial Equality (CRE) and the Equal Opportunities Commission (EOC) are appointed after consultation with the CBI. The CBI is represented on numerous Whitehall committees, and involved in all-party parliamentary groups. At an international level, it participates in the Union of Industrial and Employers' Confederations of Europe and the United Nations International Labour Organisation (ILO). In 1992 the CBI had a staff of 325, and an income of £16.8 million, 65 per cent of which came from members' subscriptions.

Trades Union Congress

The other main British peak group is the TUC. In 1994 there were 68 unions affiliated to the TUC, with a total of 7.6 million members—representing about four-fifths of all union members in Britain. The TUC, which describes itself as 'an independent association of unions', says its main aim is '. . . to help unions achieve things together which they could not do alone'. It draws up common policies and promotes and publicises them. It makes representations to government, to employers and, increasingly, to international bodies such as the EU. Among the bodies on which the TUC is represented are ACAS, CRE, and EOC (see above); it is also affiliated to the European Trade Union Confederation (ETUC) and the ILO. Its total income in 1992 was £9.6 million, £9.5 million of which came from members.

The Scottish TUC (STUC) had 53 affiliated unions in 1994, with a total affiliated membership of 768,183. Trade unions with membership in Scotland and other parts of Britain usually affiliate to both the TUC and the STUC; a few unions wholly confined to Scotland are affiliated only to the STUC. In 1994, 50 TUC-affiliated unions with members in Wales were represented on the Wales TUC, which is part of the regional council structure of the TUC.

Trade Unions

In 1991 there were 290 unions, with 9.5 million members. According to the Labour Force Survey, 37 per cent of all employees in Britain were union members in that year, although the regional figure for Northern Ireland was 47 per cent. The main concerns of trade unions are the welfare of their members, particularly wages and working conditions, but unions are also concerned with other issues affecting their industries, such as training, education and new technology, as well as social issues including racial and sexual equality.

Union Membership and Finance

While some British unions have a only a few hundred members, others have hundreds of thousands of members.

The total income in 1992 of the ten largest unions ranged from £75.8 million (NALGO) to £11.8 million (NUT). The total income of all unions in 1992 was £623 million, with £517 million of the total deriving from membership contributions. The average annual member's contribution in 1992 was £57.99. Fifty-one unions had political funds in 1992, and a total of £15.5 million was contributed by 5.6 million members; 1.1 million members claimed exemption from paying into their union's political fund.

Britain's Ten Largest Trade Unions

The following are Britain's ten largest unions, according to number of members. They are affiliated to the TUC except where indicated; the abbreviation and founding date are given in the first bracket, membership in the second bracket; * denotes the existence of a political fund:

1. UNISON (1993). Formed by a merger of the Confederation of Health Service Employees (COHSE), the National Union of Public Employees (NUPE) and the National and Local Government Officers Association (NALGO) (1,486,984).*

2. Transport and General Workers Union (TGWU, 1922). Over 75 separate unions have been incorporated into the TGWU, which represents transport and factory workers, dockers and clerks (1,036,996).*

3. GMB (1991). Formerly the General, Municipal, Boilermakers' and Allied Trades Union. Represents unskilled and semi-skilled workers in engineering, building and service industries (799,101).*

4. Amalgamated Engineering and Electrical Union (AEEU, 1992). Formed by a merger of the Electrical, Electronic Telecommunications and Plumbing Union (EETPU) and the Amalgamated Engineering Union (AEU). Represents skilled and unskilled engineering and construction workers (884,463).*

5. Manufacturing Science Finance (MSF, 1988). Represents manufacturing workers and white-collar workers in banking, insurance, NHS, education and voluntary sector (552,000).*

7. Union of Shop, Distributive and Allied Workers (USDAW, 1947). Members are mainly women in retail, wholesale and service sectors (316,491).*

8. Royal College of Nursing of the UK (RCN, 1916); not TUC-affiliated (293,193).

9. Graphical, Paper and Media Union (269,881).*

10. National Union of Teachers (213,656).

Professional Bodies

There are a number of bodies representing the 'professions', such as medicine, dentistry and teaching, which are traditionally thought of as professional associations, but which are officially classified as trade unions, such as the British Medical Association, the British Dental Association, the NUT, and the Association of University Teachers. The former two are not affiliated to the TUC while the latter two are. Professional associations tend to have the object of promoting public welfare in general through the practice of their profession, as well as promoting the welfare of their members.

Employers' Associations

In 1992 there were 245 employers' associations in Britain, with a total membership of 279,689. The total gross income of employers' associations in 1992 was £180.1 million. No associations maintained a political fund.

Membership and Function

Sectional pressure groups do not need a numerically large membership to carry weight; they can be significant because they have a high member-to-potential-member ratio. Around 75 per cent of Britain's doctors belong to the British Medical Association (BMA), which has more than 80,000 members. The BMA has a prominent role in matters relating to medicine, particularly the Government's policy on the National Health Service (NHS).

A number of the professional associations control the training and examinations for their professions, and operate a monopoly in their profession which is sanctioned by the Government. The level of members' knowledge and expertise means that they are essential participants in the process of advice and consultation with the Government on tribunals and advisory bodies.

Examples of Sectional Organisations in Commerce, Finance, Industry and the Professions

(Membership figures are for British individuals, except where indicated.)

Commerce

Association of British Chambers of Commerce (ABCC, 1890)—represents local and national business (70,000 firms are represented through 99 affiliated chambers of commerce).

Co-operative Union Ltd (1869)—represents the British Co-operative Movement (85 co-operative organisations).

Northern Ireland Chamber of Commerce and Industry (NICCI, 1783)—promotes the interests of businesses (906 firms).

Road Haulage Association Ltd (RHA, 1945)—represents the interests of British hauliers (11,500 firms).

Scottish Chambers of Commerce (1946)—represents the chambers of commerce to government (18 chambers; 8,000 firms).

Finance

British Insurance and Investment Brokers' Association (BIIBA, 1977)—represents the interests of registered insurance brokers and independent financial intermediaries (3,700 firms).

Institute of Bankers in Scotland (1875; 12,500).

Institute of Chartered Accountants in England and Wales (ICA, 1880)—the professional body for accountants (84,178); also the ICA of Scotland (1854) and in Ireland (1888).

Industry

Building Employers Confederation (BEC, 1878)—represents the construction industry in Britain (9,000 firms).

British Institute of Management (BIM, 1947)—promotes professional management (60,000; 4,000 firms).

Confederation of British Industry (CBI, 1965)—promotes the prosperity of British industry (250,000 firms).

Dairy Trade Federation Ltd (DTF, 1933)—negotiates milk purchase and distribution, and dairy employees' wages (four member associations).

Engineering Employers' Federation (EEF, 1896)—represents employers in the engineering industry (5,000 firms).

Institute of Directors (IOD, 1903)—brings the experience of business leaders to bear on public affairs (33,000).

National Farmers Union of England and Wales (NFU, 1908)—represents the interests of self-employed and employer farmers in England and Wales (110,000). Farmers in different parts of Britain are represented by the Farmers' Union of Wales (FUW, 1955; 12,000), the National Farmers' Union of Scotland (NFUS, 1913; 14,000), and the Ulster Farmers Union (UFU, 1918; 11,500).

Newspaper Publishers Association Ltd (NPA, 1906)—represents the interests of English national newspaper publishers (12 firms).

Society of Motor Manufacturers and Traders Ltd (SMMT, 1902)—promotes the British motor industry (1,600 firms).

Professions

Advertising Association (AA, 1926)—represents the interests of the advertising business (29 organisations, representing 3,000 companies).

Association of County Councils (ACC, 1974)—represents county councils in England and Wales (46 county councils).

Association of District Councils (ADC, 1973)—represents district councils and maintains standards of public service (332 non-metropolitan district councils in England and Wales).

Association of Local Authorities of Northern Ireland (ALANI, 1973)—acts on behalf of city, borough and district councils (19 district councils).

Association of Metropolitan Authorities (AMA, 1974)—represents the interests of English metropolitan authorities (87 authorities).

British Dental Association (BDA, 1880; 15,269).

British Medical Association (BMA, 1832)—services the medical profession and promotes public health (83,840).

Convention of Scottish Local Authorities (COSLA, 1975)—represents local authorities in Scotland (65 authorities).

Institution of Civil Engineers (ICE, 1818; 52,437).

Institution of Mechanical Engineers (IMechE, 1847; 66,000).

Royal Institute of British Architects (RIBA, 1834)—the promotion of civil architecture (22,333).

Royal Institution of Chartered Surveyors (RICS, 1868; 77,909).

Promotional Groups

A promotional pressure group is an organisation with a shared view or belief which is usually about a single public issue. It campaigns to provide information about its cause, and gain public support. The group aims to change public policy in favour of the view it promotes, and to campaign against policies it considers are not beneficial.

While some promotional groups like the National Trust or the Royal Society for the Prevention of Cruelty to Animals seem to have become a permanent part of British life, many promotional pressure groups tend to be of a more temporary nature than sectional groups. The groups are voluntary, and their campaigns may last for a few months or years before the group disbands. It is therefore difficult to calculate how many promotional groups there are in Britain. Directories such as *The Voluntary Agencies Directory* or the *Directory of British Associations* indicate that there are between 1,000 and 2,000 groups, but not all are pressure groups; there are also a great number which are active at a local level.

Promotional groups campaign on a wide range of causes, including aspects of politics, society, education, religion, health, social welfare, the environment, conservation, defence, and animal welfare. Some groups have an extremely large membership, such as the National Trust (over 2 million), the Royal Society for the Protection of Birds (840,000), and the National Federation of Anglers (285,000). A more typical membership size is around 1,000, and many groups are much smaller. Membership size can be important, because a large number or high 'density' of supporters will strengthen the authority of a pressure group. This also helps government departments involved in the consultation process to assess how representative a particular pressure group is.

Local Groups

As well as the above organisations which have a nationwide base, there are many promotional groups which focus on a local issue. For example, People Against the River Crossing (PARC) was set up to campaign against plans to build a road through the ancient Oxleas Wood in south London. In protest against plans in 1992 to close a number of coal mines, a range of local groups, such as the North Staffordshire Miners' Wives Action Group, was formed. The Save Bart's Campaign was set up to fight the proposed closures at St Bartholomew's Hospital in the City of London. These essentially local groups, formed either in response to a local problem, or as a local response to a national situation, do not generally outlive their campaign once it has finished. However, some local groups, such as tenants' and ratepayers' associations, which have more of the characteristics of sectional groups, are set up on a more permanent basis.

Finance

Promotional pressure groups often have their roots in charities, and their financial support comes from public donations and membership subscriptions. Promotional groups which express the views or have the backing of a sector of business or society—for example, the tobacco industry or a religious denomination—may benefit financially from such support. Some promotional groups (for example, in the area of social affairs), not only campaign for a cause, but also provide some form of practical service and receive grants from the appropriate government department. In 1992–93 the Government made grants to voluntary organisations totalling almost £4,000 million. (Most of this consisted of payments to voluntary housing associations through the Housing Corporation;

the rest went directly to voluntary organisations.) In 1992–93 the Overseas Development Administration (a government department) made a grant to Oxfam of £8.5 million and £16.9 million to Christian Aid. The Department of Health made a grant of £612,000 to Alcohol Concern while the Northern Ireland Department of Health and Social Services grant to Age Concern was £125,520.

International Groups
There are also groups based in Britain which campaign for the improvement of the lives of people who live abroad, particularly in developing countries, for example, Oxfam and Save the Children Fund. In addition, there are international friendship groups, and those working for the improvement of relations between Britain and a particular foreign country, for example, the Franco-British Society and the Britain-Zimbabwe Society. (For a list of examples of promotional groups, see Appendix.)

Pressure Groups and Political Parties

Although there are some similarities between pressure groups and political parties—both, for example, seek to introduce or change policies—there is also a clear distinction. Promotional groups usually campaign over a single cause, and interest groups promote a range of causes relevant to particular sections of society. On the other hand, political parties produce manifestos which put forward policies according to their political beliefs on *all* areas of government which are intended to be relevant to the whole of British society. (Some political parties, such as Plaid Cymru in Wales, the Scottish National Party and the Northern Ireland parties, generally campaign in only part of Britain.)

Pressure groups do not generally put forward candidates in elections, although many Labour Party parliamentary candidates are sponsored by trade unions (see p. 31). Nevertheless, there are often 'single-issue' candidates in local government elections, representing, for example, a cause relating to the local area. In general elections it is not unusual for candidates campaigning for single causes, such as capital punishment or noise abatement, to stand alongside candidates from the mainstream parties. Such candidates seldom receive many votes: they stand not with the hope of winning but in order to gain publicity.

Political parties seek to win political power, whereas pressure groups aim to influence those who are in power, rather than to exercise the responsibility of government and to legislate. MPs and local councillors as individuals, and political parties as a whole, are accountable to the electorate and must seek to persuade voters to support them at an election. While there is legislation governing the way trade unions function—for example, the holding of ballots over industrial action, and on whether members want to contribute to a political fund—pressure groups and their representatives are not publicly accountable in the way that politicians are.

There is an interrelationship between pressure groups and political parties, particularly in policy-making. For example, ideas put forward in the 1980s by the Institute of Economic Affairs are often regarded as having influenced some of the policies of the Conservative Government, including, for example, the abolition of the Manpower Services Commission, and plans for railway privatisation. The left-of-centre think-tank, the Institute for Public Policy Research, has sought to contribute to Labour Party policy.

Trade Unions

There is a close link between the Labour Party and the trade unions, which are sectional pressure groups representing employees. The Labour Party grew out of the British labour movement (see p. 11), and although the TUC is not affiliated to the Labour Party, they have worked together on policy, for example, the joint TUC-Labour Party paper of 1986, *People at Work: New Rights, New Responsibilities.* In 1993, 29 unions were affiliated to the Labour Party.

Much of Labour Party finance, particularly for election expenses, comes from the political funds of affiliated trade unions. In 1991 there were 52 unions with political funds. But not all trade unions with political funds are affiliated to the Labour Party, and trade union members are entitled to exempt themselves from contributions to a political fund.

Trade union members have a wide variety of political allegiance. For example, in the 1992 election, according to a MORI opinion poll, 47 per cent of trade union members voted for the Labour Party, 30 per cent voted for the Conservative Party, and 19 per cent voted for the Liberal Democrats.

A number of proposals to reform the relationship between the Labour Party and the trade unions are currently under discussion.

Business Interests

There are also links between business interests and political parties, particularly the Conservative Party, although the links between sectional pressure groups representing employers and the Conservative Party are not as clearly defined as the links between the Labour Party and the trade unions; the CBI, for example, has a policy of political neutrality. Business groups have no formal say over party policy. However, many Conservative MPs have traditionally had a background in business, industry or finance, and a significant proportion of Conservative Party funds has derived from donations by private companies. Under the Companies Act 1967 such companies are required to disclose the amounts of contributions above £200 made to political party funds. Less often, company donations are made to the Labour Party, and to smaller parties such as the Liberal Democrats. Employers' associations are entitled to hold political funds, but in 1991 none did so.

Pressure Groups and Parliament

Lobbying Mps and Lords

The Houses of Parliament are Britain's main political forum and law-making assembly.[2] Government ministers and Opposition spokesmen and women are normally appointed from the ranks of MPs; a few are members of the House of Lords. It is natural that pressure groups—and individual constituents—should seek to influence members of both Houses. This process of approaching MPs or Lords, persuading them to act on behalf of a cause, and enabling them to do so by providing advice and information, is called lobbying. It is a form of pressure group activity which has substantially increased in recent years.

An individual citizen can contact his or her MP by letter or telephone, or arrange to meet, to express their views on an issue in the hope of gaining the MP's support. This often takes place when MPs hold 'surgeries', where they meet individual constituents in their constituencies and attempt to tackle their problems. A common pressure group tactic is to ask members of the public to write to their MP about an issue, such as the Sunday trading laws, or the plight of political prisoners in particular countries, in order to raise awareness and persuade the MP to support the cause.

In a mass lobby a large number of people gather outside Parliament to put forward their views to their Mps. In January

[2]For further details, see *Parliament* (Aspects of Britain: HMSO, 1994).

1993, for example, several hundred people took part in a lobby organised by the pressure group National Black Caucus against the Asylum and Immigration Appeals Bill. Their concerns focused on new measures relating to the right of a non-British citizen to appeal against refusal by an immigration official to grant entry to Britain.

MPs' Interests

The parliamentary convention that MPs should declare an interest, when appropriate, became a rule of the House of Commons in May 1974, according to which '. . . a Member shall disclose any relevant pecuniary interest or benefit of whatever nature, whether direct or indirect, that he may have had, may have or be expecting to have'. In addition, a 'Register of Members' Interests' was set up, to '. . . provide information of any pecuniary interest or other material benefit which a Member may receive which may be thought to affect his conduct as a Member or influence his actions, speeches or vote in Parliament'. The Register is updated annually. Registration of an interest is additional to the requirement that MPs declare their interests when taking part in a debate in the Commons. Where there is a breach of the rules on declaring an interest, the House of Commons Select Committee on Members' Interests rec- ommends to the House an appropriate course of action. Sanctions can be severe, including suspension from the House. There is no register for members of the House of Lords, although there is a long-standing custom that members always speak 'on their hon- our'.

Sponsoring MPs

The trade unions sponsor a large number of Labour Party parlia- mentary candidates, by providing financial help with general election expenses, as well as making annual payments to the constituency parties of sponsored Labour MPs. Of the 269 Labour MPs elected at the 1992 general election, 165 (61 per cent) were sponsored. The largest number of Labour MPs sponsored by a single union was 38 by the TGWU; a total of 15 unions sponsored Labour MPs. In the past, some Conservative MPs were sponsored, for example, by the NFU, but this no longer takes place.

Parliamentary candidates have to register sponsorship in excess of 25 per cent of their election expenses, as well as any sponsorship they receive once elected or re-elected to the Commons. The Labour Party, under the terms of its Hastings Agreement on sponsorship, does not allow an affiliated organisation to pay more than 80 per cent of a candidate's election expenses, or more than £600 a year to a constituency party in a 'borough constituency' or £750 in a 'county constituency'. In the *Register of Members' Interests* published in December 1992, typical declarations by Labour MPs showed a figure of around £2,000 paid towards election expenses by their sponsoring union, and an annual donation of £3,600 to the constituency party.

Employing MPs

Many MPs, particularly Conservatives, have links with business, often through company directorships. They may also be employed as parliamentary advisers or consultants to pressure groups or companies. A much smaller number of Labour MPs and members of the smaller parties are directors or consultants. The directorships held by MPs are usually in a non-executive capacity; MPs are required to register them if they are remunerated, although they do not have to declare the amount of the payment.

MPs also act as parliamentary consultants to a wide range of sectional and promotional pressure groups. As a consultant, an MP might be expected to give information and advice about relevant parliamentary business, and speak on behalf of the interests concerned in a debate. Any such employment must be registered in the published Register of Members' Interests (see p. 31) and must be declared in the course of any relevant speech in the House. A random selection of those mentioned in the Register in 1992 included the British Field Sports Society, the Musicians' Union, the Association of University Teachers, the Music Industries Association, the Turkish Cypriot Association of the United Kingdom, the Police Superintendents' Association of England and Wales, the Chartered Society of Physiotherapists, and the International Fund for Animal Welfare.

Parliamentary Lobbyists

Groups can bring pressure to bear on both Houses through the use of parliamentary lobbyists. Many pressure groups employ full-time parliamentary workers or liaison officers, whose job is to develop contacts with MPs or Lords sympathetic to their cause, and to brief them when issues affecting the group are raised in Parliament.

There are also public relations and political consultancy firms specialising in lobbying Parliament and Government. Such firms are employed by pressure groups—as well as by British and overseas companies and organisations—to monitor parliamentary business, and to promote their clients' interests where they are affected by legislation and debate.

A number of MPs receive payments for political consultancy from public relations companies, or for acting as parliamentary advisers to promotional and sectional pressure groups. According to *Public Relations Consultancy 1992*, a directory published by the Public Relations Consultants Association, pressure group clients of PR companies included the Royal Society for the Prevention of Cruelty to Animals, the British Battery Manufacturers' Association, the Institute of Motorcycling, and the World Wide Fund for Nature.

Government ministers are not permitted to be employed by outside interests.

Register of Lobbyists

The increase in recent years of parliamentary lobbying has pro-. voked concern both inside and outside the Houses of Parliament. In a report published in July 1991, the House of Commons Select Committee on Members' Interests recommended that the House establish a 'Register of Professional Lobbyists'. The report noted: 'There has been a considerable growth in the business of political and parliamentary consultancy, particularly over the last decade. Very large sums of money, in total, are involved . . . Any democratic institution must be particularly vigilant to ensure that its actions do not become subject to improper pressure or even to allow the suspicion to arise that such pressure is being exerted.' (By April 1994 no decision had yet been made on this.)

Legislation

The business of legislation in Parliament provides opportunities for pressure groups to influence the way laws are made or amended, and to play a role in introducing new laws. The Queen's Speech at the annual state opening of Parliament outlines the legislation the Government intends to introduce in the new parliamentary session. It provides pressure groups with advance notice of legislation which may affect their interests. They may be already aware of the Government's plans for legislation from elections manifestos, Green Papers, White Papers, departmental working groups, or reports from departmental inquiries.

Bills have three readings in the House of Commons.[3] The first reading is a formal introduction of the Bill. On the second reading, the House discusses the principles of the Bill; this may be an opportunity for pressure groups to ask MPs to raise issues during the debate. The Bill goes to a standing committee after the second reading, and then returns to the House for final debate and approval at the report stage and third reading. Approximately the same process is repeated in the House of Lords. Finally, the Bill goes before the Monarch to receive the Royal Assent before becoming law.

During the committee stage, when the Bill normally goes to an all-party standing committee of MPs for detailed scrutiny, pressure groups often have the greatest opportunity to influence legislation. A strategy commonly adopted by pressure groups is to make contact with committee members sympathetic to their aims. The pressure group then briefs the MPs with suggested amendments to the legislation—together with supporting arguments—which it feels will benefit the cause of the group.

There may well be a number of pressure groups, representing different or opposing interests, seeking to exert influence at this stage. For example, during the committee stage of the Police and Criminal Evidence Act 1984, groups involved in providing briefings for MPs included Liberty: the National Council for Civil Liberties, the Children's Legal Centre, the Prison Officers' Association, and the Police Federation of England and Wales. Sometimes pressure

---

[3]For further information, see *Parliament* (Aspects of Britain: HMSO, 1994).

groups sharing common ground will form a temporary alliance. For example, during the passage of the Data Protection Act 1984, the British Medical Association, Justice, and the Law Society among others, co-operated in pooling information and proposing amendments.

The involvement of pressure groups at the committee stage has advantages for both MPs and pressure groups. MPs may not have enough time to devote to considering all the detailed aspects of a Bill, while pressure groups can provide information and expertise, with the opportunity of promoting amendments beneficial to their cause. When the Bill enters the committee stage in the House of Lords, pressure groups have similar opportunities to press for amendments (they also have a role in shaping delegated legislation—see p. 44).

Private Members' Bills

Pressure groups can also exert influence through Private Members' Bills. These are public Bills initiated by backbench MPs or Lords, and can be introduced to either House by various means although few become Acts. Successful Private Members' Bills tend to be those which do not follow party political lines, and are able to gain cross-party support. A well-known example of a law which started as a Private Member's Bill is the Chronically Sick and Disabled Persons Act 1970, introduced by the Labour MP, Alf Morris. Subjects for Private Members' Bills are often suggested by pressure groups, many of whom have ready-drafted legislation waiting to be sponsored by MPs or Lords. Private Members' Bills are also introduced by backbench MPs as a means of drawing attention to an issue, which may also have been promoted by a pressure group.

Raising Issues in Parliament

There are other ways through which pressure groups may exert influence on Parliament:

—MPs and Lords have a number of ways of formally asking questions of government ministers. The most common of these is through parliamentary questions. In the 1991-92 parliamentary session, MPs tabled 18,433 questions, the majority of which received written replies. Pressure groups often approach MPs to ask parliamentary questions as a means of gaining information from the Government and of drawing public attention to an issue.

—Early Day Motions are motions for debate printed on the daily House of Commons order paper. These are sponsored by one or more MPs, who in turn ask other MPs to add their signatures. Although the motion is never debated, this is another way of drawing attention to an issue; Early Day Motions are often suggested to MPs by pressure groups.

—Pressure groups also orchestrate public petitions as a form of protest against government policy, or to call for action. If the petition is to be presented in Parliament, it must be worded according to House of Commons or House of Lords rules, and be presented by an MP or Lord in the appropriate House.

Non-legislative Parliamentary Committees

As well as the standing committees which consider legislation, there are several other types of parliamentary committees. Select committees are set up on a statutory basis, while others are unofficial. In both cases, pressure groups have an opportunity to influence MPs.

Select Committees

Parliamentary select committees operate on either a permanent or an *ad hoc* basis, and usually deal with areas for which a government department is responsible. There are committees, for example, on Public Accounts, Home Affairs, Trade and Industry and European Community legislation. Their membership reflects the party strengths in the House of Commons, and their task is to investigate the working of relevant areas of public policy.

As well as summoning government ministers and civil servants to give evidence, the committees often hear evidence from representatives of pressure groups. For example, in February 1993 representatives of the British Paper and Board Industry Foundation gave evidence to the House of Commons Trade and Industry Select Committee on the threat to the British paper industry posed by German competitors. In the same month, the Commons Home Affairs Select Committee heard evidence from representatives of the Association of Chief Police Officers, the Police Superintendents' Association of England and Wales, and the Police Federation of England and and Wales, on the issue of dealing with juvenile offenders; and the Commons Health Select Committee heard evidence from the National Association of Health Authorities and Trusts about payment for care in the community.

Unofficial Committees

There is a large number of unofficial All-Party and parliamentary groups at Westminster consisting of members of both Houses, and reflecting the interests and concerns of backbenchers. There are currently over 130 subject groups, such as the ASH (Action on Smoking and Health) Group, the Cable and Satellite TV Group and the Penal Affairs Group, and over 80 country groups, such as the Tibet Group, or the Bangladesh Group. Many of the committees have close links with sectional and promotional pressure groups, which are able to provide information and assistance, and have the opportunity of influencing MPs. For example, the ASH group takes its name from the anti-smoking pressure group. These committees are often supported by workers from the relevant pressure groups, who help in the organisation of meetings at Westminster, and other activities. The research assistant of the All-Party Disablement Group is from the Royal Association for Disability and Rehabilitation (RADAR). The All-Party Chemical Industry Group's administration secretary is based at the Chemical Industries Association. The administation secretary of the All-Party Motor Industry Group is based at the headquarters of the Society of Motor Manufacturers and Traders. Pressure groups also have connections with the single-party committees of backbench MPs, particularly in providing information.

Pressure Groups and Government

The Growth of Government and Pressure Groups

At the start of this century, the areas in public life for which the Government was responsible were largely limited to finance and taxation, defence, law and order, and foreign relations. Beyond these areas, government departments had relatively little involvement in the lives of ordinary British citizens.

Since then, two major factors have brought about a greatly increased role for Government. During the two world wars, and the inter-war economic depression, it intervened to a far greater extent in the management and direction of the economy. The second factor has been the growth of the Welfare State, particularly in the aftermath of the second world war, with state programmes to provide health care, unemployment and sickness benefits, and pensions.

There are now around 20 government departments, with responsibilities including health, social security, education, employment, trade, transport and the environment—in addition to the older ministries, such as HM Treasury, the Home Office, and the Foreign and Commonwealth Office. The number of civil servants has grown from 61,000 in 1914 to more than half a million. Central government expenditure in 1993–94 was £166.4 million, almost half Britain's gross domestic product, and it has been estimated that 30 per cent of the population derives its main income from the Government in the form of a pension or social security benefit.

A photocall for the launch of the NSPCC's Justice for Children campaign.

The National Union of Teachers' annual conference.

Dispensing beer at a real ale festival. The Campaign for Real Ale (CAMRA) promotes the brewing and sale of traditional draught beer.

Michael Shersby, MP, speaking at the annual conference of the Police Federation of England and Wales. Mr Shersby acts as parliamentary consultant to the Federation.

Banners depicting 30 years of Amnesty 'prisoners of conscience' at an Amnesty International anniversary rally.

A demonstration by the Campaign for Nuclear Disarmament.

A peaceful demonstration by the League against Cruel Sports at a Boxing Day hunt meet.

Union of Muslim Organisations (UMO): the Annual Meeladun Nabi SAWS Dinner at which guests included Sir Teddy Taylor, MP and Jack Straw, MP.

This growth has been accompanied by an increase in the number and scope of pressure groups. As the Government has taken on responsibility for more areas of public life, so pressure groups have sprung up to campaign on behalf of particular groups of citizens, such as children, single parent families, disabled people, ethnic and social minorities, as well as about the environment, and consumer issues.

Pressure groups themselves may also play a part in increasing the range of government responsibilities, by calling for new ministries to deal with an issue of concern. For example, in March 1993 the CBI recommended that the Government should produce a Green Paper on future options for the Department of Employment and the Department for Education. One possibility would be the creation of a department responsible for compulsory education up to 16 years, and a new department responsible for all post-16 education and training.

Consultation

The principle of consultation to gain the consent and co-operation of as wide a range of organisations as possible, and ensure the smooth working of laws and regulations, plays an important part in the relationship between government departments and interested groups.

In some instances a department is under legal obligation to consult interested groups. Ministers at the Ministry of Agriculture, Fisheries and Food are obliged by the Agriculture Act 1947 to 'consult with such bodies of persons as appear to them to represent the interests of producers in the agricultural industry'.

Members of interest groups have direct expertise, and an awareness of what is practicable, and can give advice and information to civil servants engaged in preparing policy or legislation. In return, the pressure groups have the opportunity to express their opinions directly to the Government. The contacts between civil servants and pressure group representatives may be relatively informal—by letter or telephone—or more formal, through involvement in working parties or by giving evidence to committees of inquiry.

Government departments and pressure groups active in the same area of public policy often share the same broad goals—such as the provision of free health care, or the growth and development of British industry—and have contact on a basis of co-operation. However, that is not always the case. For example, in 1950–51 the British Iron and Steel Federation refused to co-operate with the Attlee administration after the nationalisation of the iron and steel industries. In 1971 the TUC refused to co-operate on legislation and other matters with the Heath Government over its reforms of industrial relations law. The 1970s in particular were marked by industrial disputes between trade unions and employers in the nationalised industries. In the 1980s the British Medical Association conducted a campaign against the Thatcher administration's planned reforms of the NHS, and the National Union of Mineworkers (NUM) was involved in a strike in 1984-85 over pit closures.

Extent of Consultation
The Department of Employment publishes a directory of around 550 employers' associations, trade unions and other organisations. This seeks '. . . to provide comprehensive lists of United Kingdom organisations whose objects include the negotiation of, or making of recommendations on, wages and working conditions, or which

provide representatives on organisations which are so concerned'. The Department of Transport Vehicle Safety Division in 1980 consulted more than 620 bodies about changes in legislation. A smaller department, ECGD (Export Credits Guarantee Department), maintained a list of 37 organisations in 1986 with which it had regular consultations. These included the Association of the British Pharmaceutical Industry, the Chemical Industries Association, the CBI, the Engineering Industries Association, Lloyds of London, the London Chamber of Commerce and Industry, the Sino-British Trade Association, the Society of Motor Manufacturers and Traders, and the West Africa Shippers Association.

Green Papers and White Papers

Before a government Bill reaches the House of Commons, it will normally have passed through a process of consultation and drafting following the publication of Green Papers and White Papers. For example, the Courts and Legal Services Act 1990 began with the publication of three government Green Papers of draft legislation in January 1989 on the organisation of the legal profession, contingency fees and conveyancing. One of these papers, *The Work and Organisation of the Legal Profession*, said that the Government would '... welcome comment from as broad a range of opinion as possible ...', and gave a deadline of 2 May 1989 for comments to be received by the Lord Chancellor's Department. At the next stage of legislation, the White Paper, *Legal Services: A Framework for the Future*, was presented to Parliament on 19 July 1989 by the Lord Chancellor. As well as the Government's proposals for legislation, the White Paper included an analysis of the 2,050 responses to the Green Paper, of which 5 per cent were from solicitors' representative bodies, 48 per cent from individual solicitors and solicitors' firms, 13 per cent from barristers, 3 per cent from the judiciary, 2 per cent from other groups including the National Association of Citizens Advice Bureaux, and 25 per cent from the public. Their responses were summarised in a 30-page annex, and another section compared the clauses of the Green Paper with the proposals of the White Paper.

Delegated Legislation

Government departments are responsible for drafting legislation, and putting that legislation into operation once it has been made an Act of Parliament. They are also responsible for putting into effect Statutory Instruments, or delegated legislation. While the broad principles of the legislation are established by Parliament, Acts often have enabling clauses which permit the Minister to issue orders and regulations at a later stage. Consultation between government departments and interested groups is sometimes mandatory. A survey of the Department of Trade and Industry in 1981 showed that of around 60 Acts under which Statutory Instruments were made, mandatory consultation was required in about 20 cases. The Health and Safety at Work Act 1974 requires the Health and Safety Commission—a public body under the Department of Employment—to consult 'appropriate organisations' before submitting proposals for making regulations under the Act. In one particular instance—the prevention of damage to hearing from noise at work—the Commission sent out draft proposals in 1987 to interested organisations in industry. Their responses had to be returned by the end of June 1988. The following year, 1989, the Commission, after 'widespread consultation' with industry, published regulations on noise at work, which set out the legal duties of employers and equipment designers and manufacturers for the prevention of damage to hearing at work. Even where consultation is not required by law, it will often take place before delegated legislation is prepared.

Working Groups

Pressure group representatives are involved in the work of departmental committees and working groups, which includes discussing policy alongside civil servants. They are able to provide information based on their own research as well as practical experience of the area in question. For example, in 1991 the Social Services Inspectorate, within the Department of Health, published *The Right To Complain*, giving guidance on complaints procedures relating to legislation on community care and children. The three working groups involved in the document included representatives from the National Council for Voluntary Organisations, the Association of County Councils, the Carers National Association, A Voice for the Child in Care, the Association of Metropolitan Authorities, Age Concern, the National and Local Government Officers' Association, as well as civil servants from the Department of Health.

In the 1980s the Department of Trade and Industry financed a scheme to evaluate the use of computers in general medical practice. The scheme's Project Evaluation Group, which published its report *General Practice Computing* in 1985, comprised five civil servants, three representatives from the BMA, two from the Royal College of General Practitioners, and a representative from the Medical Research Council.

Departmental Reviews

In preparing policy, government departments may carry out reviews and, in doing so, seek advice from groups and individuals outside the department. This may provide an opportunity for pressure groups to influence the thinking and decision-making of the departments concerned. In 1986 the Treasury published a multi-departmental review of competitive tendering and contracting for services in government departments, called *Using Private Enterprise*. The report acknowledged the 'help and advice' received from more than 30 individuals, firms and organisations, including the British Stationery and Office Products Federation, the Council of Civil Service Unions and the Institute of Personnel Management. The report also carried written evidence from the Council of Civil Service Unions and the Joint Co-ordinating Committee for Government Industrials, both of which were critical of contracting out.

Inquiries

Committees of Inquiry form another part of the policy-making process in which pressure groups play a part. The committees are set up by government ministers to investigate a particular area of public policy, and make recommendations on the basis of their findings. For example, in 1987 the Secretary of State for Education and Science appointed the Committee of Inquiry into the Teaching of English Language. The committee, under the chairmanship of Sir John Kingman, Vice-Chancellor of Bristol University, received written oral evidence from more than 200 individuals and organisations. The committee's report, published in 1988, stated that attention had been paid throughout the report to the mass of evidence received. The pressure groups contributing evidence included some of the local government associations, the CBI, the National Anti-Racist Group in Education, the National Association of Head Teachers, the National Association of Schoolmasters and Union of Women Teachers, the National Union of Teachers, and the Simplified Spelling Society.

Review bodies are also appointed by the Government to carry out investigations into public policy, and in doing so consult a wide range of opinion that includes pressure groups. The Review Body on Civil Justice was set up in 1985 to improve the operation of the civil justice system in England and Wales. Between February 1986 and March 1987 it sent out six consultation papers before producing its report, *Civil Justice Review*. It received evidence from more than 50 organisations representing barristers and solicitors, as well as legal pressure groups, and more than 200 other respondents, including Age Concern, the Automobile Association, the Consumers' Association, Shelter, and the TGWU.

Public Bodies

Pressure groups are involved in various ways with non-departmental public bodies, which are set up by the Government to help administer public policy. They include executive bodies, advisory bodies and tribunals. Some of these bodies are commonly known by the acronym 'quango' (quasi-autonomous non-governmental organisation). All or most of their funding is from the government department which sponsors them. The minister of the sponsoring department is accountable for the public body, and appoints its chairman or woman. Executive bodies often have a large staff and budget; advisory bodies and tribunals are much smaller organisations.

Executive Bodies

There were 369 executive bodies in 1992 including, for example, the National Portrait Gallery, Highlands and Islands Enterprise in Scotland, and the Northern Ireland Tourist Board. The boards of a number of executive bodies include nominees from pressure groups. The Health and Safety Commission, which is the responsibility of the Department of Employment, has nominees from the TUC and CBI.

Advisory Bodies

Advisory bodies are set up by ministers to give advice to them and their departments. There were 874 such bodies in 1991; examples include the Department of Health's Committee on the Ethics of Gene Therapy, the Northern Ireland Department of Education's Curriculum Council, and the Scottish Office's Historic Buildings Council. Another example is the Law Commission, which is under the Lord Chancellor's Department, and makes recommendations for changes in the law. It reported in 1989 on computer misuse, following the issue of its working paper on the subject in 1988. A number of organisations provided comments on the paper, including the British Computer Society, the CBI, the Electronic Engineering Association, the Bar Council, the Law Society Criminal Law Committee, and the Police Federation of England and Wales.

Royal Commissions

Royal Commissions are advisory bodies set up by Royal Warrant under the Government's instigation, to enquire into an issue, such as higher education or homosexuality, and make policy recommendations. Some Commissions, such as the Royal Commission on

Environmental Pollution, are set up on a long-term basis; others cease to exist once they have produced their report. The most recent example, the Royal Commission on Criminal Justice, was set up in 1991.

Representatives of pressure groups are sometimes appointed to Royal Commissions. For example, both the CBI and the TUC were represented on the Commission on the Reform of the Trade Unions and Employers' Associations (1965–68). Royal Commissions also consult interested groups and ask them to submit their opinions. The Royal Commission on Legal Services in Scotland, which reported in 1980, received evidence from 135 groups and individuals. In its report in 1983 on lead in the environment, the Royal Commission on Environmental Pollution received evidence from more than 60 organisations (for further details, see p. 65).

Administration by Pressure Groups

As well as providing information and opinions, pressure groups can also be involved in the administration of government policy. The Law Society—the representative body for solicitors—administered the Government's Legal Aid scheme until that function was taken over in 1989 by the Legal Aid Board, which is the responsibility of the Lord Chancellor's Department. The Government also makes grants to pressure groups which, as well as speaking on behalf of their members or for an issue, also provide a service. Relate: National Marriage Guidance has received grants for its advice centres, and government departments make grants to a number of pressure groups for research relating to public policy. The National Children's Bureau, for example, has received grants for research into child development, child-minding, local authority child care, and adoption.

Lobbyists and Whitehall

The recent increase in the activity of professional lobbyists in Parliament has also affected government departments. Public relations consultants offer to lobby government departments on behalf of their clients, who include pressure groups. Sometimes those who carry out the lobbying are former civil servants or politicians with an 'insider's' knowledge of the way Government works. They are able to make direct contact with the ministers and officials who are dealing with a particular issue and put their client's case. For example, Sir Trevor Lloyd-Hughes, a former journalist and civil servant who became a private information consultant on Whitehall, told the House of Commons Select Committee on Members' Interests on 8 December 1982 how he maintained relationships with government ministers and their civil service advisers on behalf of his clients. He told the Committee: 'I am trying to build the bridge of communication between those who govern and make the laws and the regulations and apply the regulations and the minister and the guys out there in industry. . . . '

Pressure Groups and the European Union

Many important policy decisions affecting Britain are now made within the EU, particularly in the areas of agriculture, the environment, trade, health and safety, and foreign policy. A wide range of pressure groups seeks to influence the main EU institutions: the European Commission, the Council of the European Union, the European Parliament and the European Court of Justice.

The Economic and Social Committee (ECOSOC) is an advisory and consultative body set up to provide a forum for pressure groups within the EU. It has 189 members nominated by the member states, and is divided into three groups—employers, workers, and representatives of other pressure groups, such as consumers and the self-employed. It gives opinions on proposed EC legislation, and can bring issues to the attention of the Commission, Parliament and Council.

While it is possible for individual pressure groups from member states to lobby the EU administration, the European Commission much prefers to deal with EU-wide pressure groups and recognises around 500 such organisations.[4] Often their membership includes countries outside the EU member states. In general, these groups aim to represent their members' interests at a European level; to monitor the EU institutions; and to provide information and advice to EU authorities.

---

[4]Further information is available from the *Directory of Pressure Groups in the European Community*—see Further Reading.

British Involvement in European Groups

Some of the largest of the European pressure groups are UNICE (employers), COPA (farmers), ETUC (trade unions), CEFIC (chemical industries) and the EBU (broadcasters).

UNICE, the Union of Industrial and Employers' Confederations of Europe, represents European business and industry to EU institutions. It has 33 member federations from 22 European countries. The President of the CBI is a member of UNICE's governing body, the Director-General is a member of its Executive Committee, and CBI representatives attend UNICE policy committees.

The TUC is affiliated to ETUC, the European Trade Union Confederation, which has affiliates from 22 countries. ETUC co-ordinates trade union representation and information on issues arising in the EU, and generally aims to promote the welfare of workers in Europe. It is one of the largest European pressure groups, with a staff of around 35 in its Brussels office, and an annual budget of around £2 million.

Examples of individual British pressure group involvement in Europe include the NFU's membership of the Committee of Agricultural Organisations in the EU (COPA); the Advertising Association's membership of the European Advertising Tripartite (EAT); and the 23 British members of the European Environmental Bureau (EEB), including Friends of the Earth, the Scottish Environment Council, and the World Wide Fund for Nature (WWF-UK).

Protests against EU Policy

Farmers and fishermen often arrange protests and demonstrations against the EU's agricultural and fisheries policies. In one example of pressure group activity, Scottish trawlermen in December 1992 blocked French trawlers using the port of Lochinver in Scotland in a protest against fishing quotas set by the Common Fisheries Policy. While the French were still entitled to fish because they had not used up their quota, the Scottish trawlers had already done so and were protesting against the system.

Other Forms of Pressure Group Campaigning

Pressure groups campaign in a number of ways which are designed to highlight issues and influence public opinion and policy.

The Media

Use of the mass media in Britain is an important part of pressure group strategy. Daily audiences for the main television news programmes number well over 10 million. The main tabloid newspapers such as *The Sun* and *Daily Mirror* have circulation figures of 3.5 million and 2.7 million respectively. Circulation for broadsheet newspapers ranges from 289,000 for the *Financial Times* to just over 1 million for *The Daily Telegraph*.

Most pressure groups have press officers who act as a point of contact for journalists wanting information, as well as arranging press releases and briefings to present the views of the group, and enabling the media to cover future events. Pressure groups are also able to provide spokesmen and women when the media want specialist commentators. They regularly organise press conferences, when journalists are invited to a meeting given by a group to make an announcement or launch a new report, as well as responding to questions from the press.

The most direct way for promotional and sectional pressure groups to use the media is through advertising. Where permitted, they can buy, or are given, advertising space in the media and on roadside billboards, in order to raise funds or campaign.

Pressure groups also seek to gain free coverage in the media by organising events which will make news, and 'stunts' which provide opportunities for spectacular photographs or television film. For example, when supporters of the Campaign for the Abolition of Angling disrupted an angling competition in Wiltshire in 1993 they arranged for a television camera crew to be present to film the protest.

Pressure groups often enlist the support and involvement of well-known public figures, to add credibility or attract public and media attention. Pop stars have taken part in concerts for Amnesty International, Rock Against Racism, and to protest on behalf of the South African President, Nelson Mandela, when he was in prison. On a local level, the actress, Dame Judi Dench, the writer, Beryl Bainbridge, and the television presenter and novelist, Melvyn Bragg, were among celebrities who took part in a campaign against proposals by the London Borough of Camden to close a number of public libraries.

There is a long tradition of engaging in public debate by writing letters or, on occasion, articles for publication in the national press, particularly in the broadsheet newspapers, which are more likely to be read by policy-makers in the Government. In one example, NHS proposals concerning the future of St Bartholomew's Hospital in the City of London were discussed in letters to the editor of *The Times* in December 1992. The letter writers included the hospital's chief executive, representatives of the Patients' Committee, the 'Save Bart's Campaign', and a member of the City of London's Court of Common Council.

Demonstrations

Aside from the mass lobbying of Parliament, pressure groups organise a variety of public demonstrations, with protestors often shouting slogans and waving placards. Demonstrations are usually at the place which is the focus of the campaign—such as the military bases used as sites for nuclear weapons, or a factory where the employees are on strike—or they may be organised as a march. Marches are generally noisy but non-violent, and are organised with the co-operation of the police; however, they can become violent, particularly when opposing groups of demonstrators clash. Gatherings of more than 50 people are not permitted within one mile of Parliament when either House is sitting.

The Courts

Pressure groups may resort to law to protect the interests of their members, or to promote a cause. In particular, disputes between employers and trade unions may be the subject of legal action. The NUM and the National Association of Colliery Overmen, Deputies and Shotfirers took legal action against British Coal in the High Court in 1993 over consultation procedures related to the planned closure of ten coalmines. The unions said British Coal had failed to consult fully, but the court ruled that the unions had been premature in bringing the action because the negotiations between the two sides had not formally broken down.

The National and Local Government Officers' Association backed the case of an employee of Stockport Metropolitan Borough Council who took legal action against her employer after developing bronchitis which she claimed was due to working in an office where her colleagues habitually smoked cigarettes. The employee won out-of-court compensation in 1993.

Promotional groups also take legal action in support of their aim. For example, members of PARC (People Against the River Crossing—see p. 25)—residents of south London living near

Oxleas Wood, through part of which the Department of Transport had planned to build a road linking up with the East London River Crossing—took action in the High Court in 1993 to appeal against the compulsory purchase of land needed for construction work. They lost the case, but the Department of Transport subsequently announced changes to its plans.

Reports and Surveys

The use of information, statistics, research data and opinion poll surveys to support an argument or campaign is an important part of pressure group campaigning. Sometimes this information is obtained through parliamentary questions. Often it derives from reports and surveys produced or commissioned by pressure groups. To maximise their impact, the results of the study are normally released to the media. For example, the Campaign for the Protection of Rural England published *The Lost Land*, a report by a land use consultant, in October 1992. This claimed that more countryside was being turned into urban land than was indicated by Department of Environment statistics. In December 1992 the National Association of Citizens Advice Bureaux (NACAB) published a report, *The Cost of Living*, based on a study of CAB clients, which argued for new legislation relating to banking and credit. Both reports received coverage in the national press.

Pressure groups employ a wide range of legal campaigning methods. Some activities, such as secondary picketing by trade unions, or striking without holding a secret ballot, have now been made illegal. Pressure group members may have strong feelings about the causes they support, which can lead to confrontation and breaking the law. For example, it is not uncommon for violence to break out—with police arrests following—at hunt meetings between members of the hunt and demonstrators opposed to blood sports. Some radical activists who are against scientific experiments on animals have taken part in raids on laboratories, and some people who are against the trade in animal fur have attacked fur shops. When such activists deliberately use violence to achieve their objects, the line between legitimate campaigning and terrorism has been crossed.

Case Study: The Campaign Against Lead In Petrol

Background

Lead is a toxic substance, with widespread use in plumbing, paint manufacture, and as an additive to petrol intended to boost its octane quality and protect engine parts from excessive wear. Scientific evidence suggesting a health risk from exposure to lead caused the United States Government to rule that from 1975 all new cars should run on lead-free petrol, and that such petrol should be available at petrol stations.

In Britain, there was public concern about the harmful effects of lead in the environment, particularly over studies suggesting a correlation between a high level of lead in the blood stream, and the low IQs of some children living in inner city areas. The pressure group, Campaign Against Lead In Petrol (CALIP), was formed in the late 1960s, and a number of newspapers ran investigative campaigns on the subject.

An EC directive was agreed in 1978, setting the maximum lead content of petrol that could be sold within the EC at 0.4 grams per litre, to be met by 1981. In 1980 the report on lead pollution by the government-sponsored Lawther working party was published. The report was not categorical about the health threat posed by low or even intermediate blood levels of lead, but recommended that the Government take steps to reduce the population's exposure to the metal. In May 1981 the Government decided to reduce the maximum permitted level of lead in petrol from 0.4 grams per litre—the level set by the EC directive—to 0.15 grams per litre, from January 1985.

The Start of CLEAR's Campaign

The idea of introducing unleaded petrol gained widespread public support in January 1982 with the establishment of the environmental pressure group CLEAR (Campaign for Lead-free Air). CLEAR had five objectives:

—the maximum limit of 0.15 grams of lead per litre of petrol should be introduced before the end of 1985;

—by 1985 all cars sold should run on lead-free petrol;

—all petrol stations should have lead-free petrol available;

—taxation on petrol should give a price advantage to lead-free petrol; and

—surveillance of the use of lead should be encouraged and enforced by law.

The start of the campaign by CLEAR significantly raised the profile of the anti-lead movement in Britain. The Chairman of CLEAR was Des Wilson, who had launched the housing pressure group Shelter in the 1960s. CLEAR had two administrative staff, and two doctors as advisers. The organisation had the backing of a wealthy businessman, Godfrey Bradman, who provided a budget of £100,000 for the campaign.

The CLEAR campaign was highly successful in mobilising public and media interest and in lobbying British and EC politicians to support the argument for introducing unleaded petrol.

Campaign Strategy

CLEAR laid the foundations of the launch by gathering information, marshalling arguments, and devising a sophisticated strategy to influence public opinion and government policy, based on the health question posed by lead. National environmental pressure groups formed a coalition to support the campaign, and by the time of the launch, CLEAR had the support of more than 130 MPs. Well-known figures, such as the environmentalist David Bellamy and trade unionist Clive Jenkins, were members of a trust formed by CLEAR to carry out research and conduct public education.

Scientific Studies

At the launch of CLEAR at a press conference in January 1982, evidence of a direct link between still births and malformations in babies and the amount of lead pollution from car exhausts was presented. Another study was cited, showing an average level of lead in children in London schools of 13 parts per million—above the level (10 parts per million) known to interfere with enzymes, but below the level (35 parts per million) accepted as safe by the Government.

Use of Media

Throughout the campaign, use of the media was a key strategic element. CLEAR held meetings in Coventry, Birmingham, Manchester, Liverpool, Leeds, Newcastle, Bristol, Southampton and Cardiff, to achieve publicity, meet local health officials, and to set up local support centres: according to Des Wilson, 'these cities were chosen because they are media centres, each with television stations covering the surrounding counties'. A succession of pieces of evidence in support of the case against lead were made public to maintain the level of publicity.

The Yellowlees Letter

At the start of February 1982 CLEAR released the text of a letter by Sir Henry Yellowlees (Chief Medical Officer at the Department of Health and Social Security) which had originally been written on 6 March 1981 to the Permanent Secretary at the Department of Education and Science. CLEAR passed the letter to *The Times*, which printed it on 8 February 1982. Sir Henry said that further evidence since the Lawther report supported the view that even at low blood levels, lead could adversely affect IQ. He thought that truly conclusive evidence might not be available, and doubted whether there was anything to be gained by waiting for further evidence. He wrote: 'There is a strong likelihood that lead in petrol is permanently reducing the IQ of many of our children. Although the reduction amounts to only a few percentage points, some hundreds of thousands of children are affected . . .'

Petrol Industry Response

Two days later *The Times* published a letter from the Managing Director of Associated Octel—a company owned by Britain's main petrol companies, and producing the organic lead compound added to motor fuels—in response to the claims for new evidence about lead and health. There was also a letter from the Director General of the United Kingdom Petrol Industry Association, on the cost to the oil industry of reducing the lead content in petrol.

CLEAR then released a report by the management consultants, Coopers and Lybrand, which Godfrey Bradman (see p. 60) had commissioned in 1981. The strongly worded report urged every reasonable precaution to be taken against lead poisoning.

Use of Parliament

On 15 February 1982 Stanley Johnson, Conservative Member of the European Parliament for the Isle of Wight and Hampshire, East, tabled a motion at the European Parliament calling for an EC directive to ensure that all cars marketed in the Community from the start of 1985 could run on lead-free petrol. The motion was prepared in collaboration with CLEAR. In the British Parliament, Labour MP Ernest Roberts asked the Prime Minister, Margaret Thatcher, for the earlier introduction of controls of lead in petrol.

Further Evidence

Friends of the Earth, one of the environmental pressure groups supporting the CLEAR campaign, published a report *Lead in Petrol: an Energy Analysis* in late February. The report said that the use of unleaded petrol would save 400,000 tonnes of oil annually in Britain—a claim which was then rejected by Associated Octel. On 7 March 1982 the MORI organisation published an opinion poll commissioned by CLEAR, in which 90 per cent of people who were questioned believed that lead in petrol was a health hazard and wanted it banned, and 77 per cent wanted action even if it meant prices rising by 'a few pence per gallon'.

Political Support

It was reported in March 1982 that over 170 MPs from different parties had signed their support for CLEAR, including 30 Conservatives. Later that month, the Royal Commission on Environmental Pollution, under the chairmanship of Professor Richard Southwood, decided to study lead pollution because of the increasing urgency surrounding the question. The level of political support for the anti-lead campaign became evident during the 1982 political party conference season. In September the Labour Party pledged to eliminate lead from petrol, and the Liberal Party approved a resolution by Des Wilson—a party member—demanding that all new cars be manufactured to run on lead-free petrol, and all petrol stations be required to supply it. In the same month, Mr Wilson said that 35 Conservative MPs were in support of a ban on lead in petrol.

Octel's Advertising Campaign

In response, Associated Octel took out full-page advertisements in the national newspapers, titled 'The health and wealth of the nation'. In them, the company said: 'Octel can state with absolute conviction that the assertions of the anti-lead campaign regarding a connection between airborne lead and health—and children's health in particular, are unsubstantiated medically or scientifically . . . The penalty of removing lead from petrol altogether would be simply enormous in cost terms, with no measurable health benefit.' Instead, the company proposed an exhaust gas filter to trap '90 per cent' of petrol's lead content.

Further Reports

In March 1983 CLEAR maintained its momentum by publishing two surveys. The first was of dust samples taken from school playgrounds and the pavements around the schools at sites in 25 urban areas, which revealed in some cases more than 5,000 parts per million of lead—above the acceptable maximum set by the Greater London Council. The second report, on the lead content of vegetables in inner city gardens, said that many vegetables contained an unsafe level of lead.

Royal Commission Recommendations

On 18 April 1983 the Royal Commission published its ninth report, *Lead in the Environment*, dealing with a wide range of uses of lead, including in petrol. In the course of a year, the Commission had received evidence from 12 government departments, more than 60 organisations and more than 40 individuals. The organisations included Associated Octel, the AA, the British Ecological Society, the British Medical Association, CLEAR, the Chemical Industries Association, Friends of the Earth, the Lead Development Association, the Paintmakers' Association, the Society of Motor Manufacturers and Traders, and the Petroleum Industry Association.

The Commission recommended that the reduction of the maximum permitted lead content of petrol to 0.15 grams per litre 'should be regarded as an intermediate stage in the phasing out of lead additives altogether', and that the Government should negotiate with the EC to secure the removal of the minimum level for lead in petrol, and agree a timetable with British oil and motor industries for the introduction of unleaded petrol, which should not exceed the price of highest grade leaded petrol by 1990 at the latest.

Government's Response

On the same day, Tom King, then Secretary of State for the Environment, told the House of Commons that the Government accepted the Commission's recommendations on lead in petrol, and proposed the EC directive be amended to remove the minimum limit it contained so as to make possible the widespread use of unleaded petrol throughout the EC. He proposed that all new petrol-engined vehicles sold in Britain would be required to run on unleaded petrol by 1990 'at the latest'. Writing in *The Times* on 19

April, Mr Wilson welcomed the Government's decision, but pressed for an earlier date than 1990 for the introduction of lead-free petrol. Since then, CLEAR has disbanded, but CALIP (the Campaign Against Lead In Petrol) continues its campaign for a total ban on lead in petrol.

Recent Developments: Unleaded Petrol

Following an initiative by the British Government, an EC directive was adopted in March 1985, requiring unleaded petrol to be made available throughout the Community from 1 October 1989, or earlier if member states wished. In Britain, the sale of unleaded petrol was permitted from the end of 1985. By October 1988, 11 per cent of Britain's petrol stations were selling unleaded petrol. By September 1993 unleaded petrol was on sale in practically all petrol stations in Britain. In March 1989 the tax differential between leaded and unleaded petrol was raised to 14p a gallon; this was raised to 16p in March 1990, when the proportion of the total price of petrol formed by tax was 60 per cent for unleaded, compared with 64 per cent for leaded. In March 1993, the Department of the Environment announced that the market share of unleaded petrol had passed the 50 per cent mark. Unleaded petrol is expected to account for over 90 per cent of petrol sales by 2000.

Since October 1990 all new cars have been manufactured to be capable of running on unleaded petrol. In compliance with EC standards, all new passenger cars sold from January 1993 have had to be equipped with catalytic converters to reduce emissions of carbon monoxide.

Reducing the lead content of petrol has produced dramatic reductions in lead emissions and airborne lead concentrations in

Britain. Since 1985 levels of airborne lead in Britain have fallen by about 70 per cent, while the annual emissions of lead from road vehicles fell from 6,500 tonnes in 1985 to 955 tonnes in 1993.

Appendix

Examples of Promotional Groups

The examples of promotional groups given below represent only a small proportion of such groups. They are chosen to illustrate the range of interests covered and are listed according to subject. The letters in the first bracket are the initials the organisation is commonly known by; these are followed by the founding date. The final bracket contains the number of members, where known; the figure is for individuals, unless stated.

Abortion

Abortion Law Reform Association (ALRA, 1936)—to promote in law and practice a woman's right to choose on abortion (1,000).

Life: Save the Unborn Child (LIFE, 1970)—to campaign against all abortion, and provide support during and after pregnancy (30,500).

National Abortion Campaign (1975)—to campaign for changes to abortion laws, and greater access to abortion (600).

Society for the Protection of Unborn Children (SPUC, 1967)—to campaign for the repeal of the 1967 Abortion Act and for positive alternatives which respect the human right to life (46,000).

Animals

British Field Sports Society (BFSS, 1930)—to promote field sports and provide information about the benefits of field sports (80,000; 2,200 firms).

British Hedgehog Preservation Society (BHPS, 1982)—to provide care and advice, and carry out research into hedgehogs (10,500 both in Britain and overseas).

Cats Protection League (CPL, 1927)—to promote the care of cats (33,000).

League Against Cruel Sports (LACS, 1924)—to campaign for the protection of animals, especially those hunted for sport (28,972).

National Canine Defence League (NCDL, 1891)—to promote the care and protection of dogs (30,000).

Royal Society for the Prevention of Cruelty to Animals (RSPCA, 1824)—to promote kindness, and prevent cruelty, to animals (20,500).

Royal Society for the Protection of Birds (RSPB, 1889)—conservation and protection of wild birds (840,000).

Scottish Society for the Prevention of Cruelty to Animals (SSPCA, 1839; 3,000); Ulster Society for the Prevention of Cruelty to Animals (USPCA, 1836; 900).

Consumer Affairs

Association for Consumer Research (1956)—maintenance and improvement of standard goods and services offered to consumers; publishes a range of magazines (705,459).

Campaign for Real Ale (CAMRA, 1971)—to promote the brewing and sale of traditional draught beer (31,000).

Cultural

British Museum Society (BMS, 1968)—to support the British Museum (8,000).

The Burns Federation—to encourage societies which honour Robert Burns, to promote Scottish language, literature, art and music (303 branches).

Elgar Society (1951)—to promote interest in Sir Edward Elgar and his music (1,050).

National Association of Decorative and Fine Arts Societies (NAD-FAS, 1968)—to promote the aesthetic education of the public, and the study of decorative and fine arts (60,000).

Defence/Disarmament

Campaign for Nuclear Disarmament (CND, 1958)—to promote disarmament and an alternative defence policy (60,000).

Mothers for Peace (1981)—to promote world peace through friendship between women and the care of their children (280).

Peace Pledge Union (1934)—to promote pacifism and non-violent solutions to conflict (1,175).

Education and Science

British Association for the Advancement of Science (BAAS, 1831)—to promote interest in science (2,500).

British Computer Society (BCS, 1957)—to provide advice to government and industry on computing (34,000).

Workers' Educational Association (WEA, 1903)—to promote adult education (180,000).

Environment/Conservation

Architectural Heritage Society of Scotland (1956)—the protection and appreciation of ancient architecture in Scotland (960 individuals; 50 firms).

Association for the Protection of Rural Scotland (APRS, 1926)—for the protection of the Scottish countryside (1,000; 89 organisations).

British Naturalists' Association (BNA, 1905)—the protection and preservation of wildlife, conservation areas and sanctuaries (5,000).

Council for the Protection of Rural England (CPRE, 1926)—to promote the preservation of the English countryside (45,000).

Friends of the Earth (FOE, 1971)—to campaign for the protection of the environment (240,000 worldwide).

Greenpeace (1971)—to protect the environment through peaceful direct action.

National Trust (NT, 1895)—the preservation of lands and buildings of natural beauty or historic interest (2,200,000); National Trust for Scotland (NTS, 1931; 234,500).

Health

Alzheimer's Disease Society (1979)—to provide relief and support for sufferers and their relatives, and to carry out research (15,000).

Action on Smoking and Health (ASH, 1971)—anti-smoking campaign (1,400).

British Diabetic Association (BDA, 1934)—to help diabetics and support research (130,000).

British Homoeopathic Association (BHA, 1902)—to promote homoeopathic medicine (5,000).

British Limbless Ex-Service Men's Association (BLESMA, 1932)—to promote the welfare of all who have lost a limb or an eye in military service (9,000).

British Red Cross Society (1870)—to aid the sick in times of war, improve public health and prevent disease (100,000).

Royal Society for the Prevention of Accidents (ROSPA, 1916)—education in accident prevention.

International

English Speaking Union of the Commonwealth (ESU, 1918)—to promote friendship between peoples of the Commonwealth and the United States (9,000 in Britain; 71,000 overseas).

Franco-British Society (1944)—encouragement of British understanding of French culture (600).

German Chamber of Industry and Commerce in the UK (1971)—to promote British-German trade (800 firms in Britain).

International Aid

Amnesty International—British Section (1961)—to campaign to promote human rights (85,000).

Catholic Fund for Overseas Development (CAFOD, 1962)—to support Catholic churches throughout the world and combat hunger, disease, poverty and injustice.

Christian Aid (1946)—to channel resources to needy areas of the world and support overseas Christian churches.

Oxfam (1942)—to relieve poverty, distress and suffering in Africa, Asia, Latin America and the Middle East.

Save the Children Fund (1919)—to promote the rights of children and influence national and international policy to the benefit of children.

Leisure

Camping and Caravanning Club Ltd (1901)—to promote camping and caravanning (200,000).

Inland Waterways Association (IWA, 1946)—to campaign for the restoration and development of Britain's navigable waterways (22,000).

Ramblers' Association (The Ramblers)—to encourage rambling and the care of the countryside (90,000).

Motoring
Automobile Association (AA, 1905)—to serve and represent the interests of motorists (6,200,000).

Royal Automobile Club Motoring Services Ltd (RAC, 1897)—to provide services to motorists and to promote the development of motoring (4,991,000).

Politics
Electoral Reform Society (1884)—to promote the adoption of pro-portional representation, and conduct elections for voluntary organisations (2,000).

Fabian Society (1884)—to conduct social and political research (4,000 Britain and overseas).

Freedom Association (1975)—to promote a wide range of citizens' freedoms (7,000).

Liberty: National Council for Civil Liberties (Liberty, 1934)—to defend and extend civil liberties (8,000).

Religion
Board of Deputies of British Jews (1760)—the representative body of Anglo-Jewry, to ensure against discrimination against British Jews.

Evangelical Alliance of Great Britain (EA, 1846)—to promote joint Christian action (30,313; 1,853 churches).

Union of Muslim Organisations of the UK and Eire (UMO, 1970)—to co-ordinate the work of over 180 affiliated Muslim organisations.

Lord's Day Observance Society (LDOS, 1831)—to preserve Sunday as a national day of rest (500).

Mothers' Union (1876)—to strengthen and preserve marriage and Christian family life (170,000).

Social Welfare

Child Poverty Action Group (CPAG, 1965)—to promote the relief of poverty among children and families with children (6,000).

Gingerbread (1970)—to promote the welfare of one-parent families (8,000).

National Association of Citizens Advice Bureaux (NACAB, 1939)—to provide free information and advice on all subjects (1,346 bureaux).

National Society for the Prevention of Cruelty to Children (NSPCC, 1884) to prevent child abuse and neglect (2,497).

Sport

Cyclists Touring Club (CTC, 1878)—the encouragement of cycling and the protection of cyclists' interests (37,000).

Football Association Ltd (FA, 1863)—promotion and organisation of Association Football in England (47 county associations; 42,000 clubs).

Football Association of Wales Ltd (1876)—administration of Association Football in Wales (91 clubs).

National Federation of Anglers (NFA, 1903)—to promote the improvement of fishery laws and the development of fishing waters; to combat river pollution (285,000).

Scottish Rugby Union (SRU, 1873; 13,500).

Addresses

Certification Office for Trade Unions and Employers' Associations, 27 Wilton Street, London SW1X 7AZ.

Confederation of British Industry, Centre Point, 103 New Oxford Street, London WC1A 1DU.

Economic and Social Committee (ECOSOC), 2 rue Ravenstein, 1000 Brussels, Belgium.

National Council for Voluntary Organisations, Regent's Wharf, 8 All Saint's Street, London N1 9RL.

Trades Union Congress, Congress House, Great Russell Street, London WC1B 3LS.

Further Reading

Pressure Groups and Government in Great Britain.
Alderman, Geoffrey.   Longman 1984

Pressure Groups and the Political System.
Brennan, Tom.   Longman 1985

Parties and Pressure Groups.
Coxall, W. N. Second edition.   Longman 1986

Politics of Pressure. Davies, Malcolm.   BBC 1985

Lobbying. Dubbs, Alf.   Pluto Press 1988

MPs for Hire. Hollingsworth, Mark.   Bloomsbury 1991

Politics UK. Jones, Bill *et al.*   Philip Allan 1991

Government and Pressure Groups in Britain.
Jordan, A.G. and Richardson, J. J.   Oxford University Press 1987

British Politics: Continuities and Change.
Kavanagh, Dennis. Second edition.   Oxford University Press 1990

Trade Union Handbook.
Marsh, Arthur. Fifth edition.   Gower 1991

A History of British Trade Unionism.
Pelling, Henry. Fifth edition.   Penguin 1992

*Directory of Pressure Groups in the European
Community.* Philip, A. B. (*ed.*)   Longman 1992

Charitable Status. Phillips, A. and Smith, K.
Fourth edition.   Directory of Social Change 1993

Organising Things. Ward, Sue.   Pluto Press 1984

Pressure: the A to Z of Campaigning in Britain.
Wilson, Des.   Heinemann 1984

Interest Groups. Wilson, Graham K.   Basil Blackwell 1990

Reports and Directories

Annual Report of the Certification Officer 1992–1993.

Central Government Grants Guide.
Fourth edition.   Directory of Social Change 1992

Centres and Bureaux. Edited by
Lindsay Sellar.   C.B.D. Research Ltd 1987

Directory of British Associations
Eleventh edition.   C.B.D. Research Ltd 1992

Political Activities by Charities.
Leaflet No CC9.   Charity Commissioners

*Public Relations Consultancy
1992.*   Public Relations Consultants Association

Register of Members' Interests. Annual   HMSO

Royal Commission on Environmental Pollution.
Ninth report: Lead in the Environment.
Cmnd. 8852 1983

The Voluntary Agencies Directory 1993-94.
Thirteenth edition.   NCVO Publications 1993

Index

Printed in the UK for HMSO.
Dd.0297893, 8/94, C30, 56–6734, 5673.